Safe to Be Me

How I Healed, Traveled, and Transformed

by Elaina Rice

Dedication
To my friends and family
that supported me
through this last year,
I can't **thank you** enough.
But I will *try*.

Table of Contents

Chapter 1: The Breaking Point: A February Morning

The February morning air pressed against the window, icy and unyielding. I sat on the edge of my bed, my breath shallow, the silence in my house was broken only by the frantic beating of my heart. My body felt—tense, heavy, as if gravity itself had turned against me. Outside, the world was waking up, but inside, it felt like I was dying.

For years, I had survived by wearing a carefully constructed mask. Each day, I stepped into the role expected of me: the high-achieving professional, the good friend, the one who always held it together. Outwardly, my life looked enviable. I had a job that paid well, survived multiple rounds of corporate reorganization, and received the kind of annual bonuses people dream about. But what looked like safety to others felt more like a gilded cage to me—a place where I was constantly shrinking, trying to fit into a mold that left no room for my true self.

I couldn't pinpoint the exact day it started, the gradual erosion of my self-worth. Maybe it was after my peer—a woman who'd given decades of her life to the company—was fired. Maybe it was the day I realized that praise only came with the expectation to do more, alone, with less support. Or maybe it was the countless small moments when I silenced my own needs, convinced myself that gratitude for what I had should be enough to quiet the growing ache inside.

But that cold February morning, it all caught up with me. As I sat frozen in my desk chair, it was as if my mind and body staged a mutiny. I couldn't muster the energy to move. My thoughts raced, a relentless loop of fear and despair: "This isn't safe. I can't do this anymore. I feel like I'm dying." The words echoed so loudly that it seemed impossible no one else could hear them.

For a moment, I considered simply disappearing—letting the darkness swallow me, ending the pain in the only way that seemed possible. But something deeper, a stubborn instinct for survival, nudged me to reach out. I remembered the therapist hotline number my company had provided months before, a resource I'd always filed away as something "for other people." My hands trembled as I dialed. When the nurse answered, all I could manage was, "I don't feel safe. I feel like I'm dying."

The words hung heavy in the air, but she didn't flinch. Her voice was gentle, steady—a lifeline in my chaos. "You're not alone," she assured me. "You've taken the right first step. Your appointment tonight will help, and we'll support you through the process of going on medical leave. What you're experiencing is real, and you deserve help."

As I hung up the phone, I felt a faint glimmer of relief—so fragile it barely registered, but there. For the first time in months, maybe years, I had admitted the truth: I was not okay. I needed help. I was no longer willing to pretend.

The nurse's promise echoed through my mind as I waited for my appointment that evening. The hours between the call and the session stretched endlessly. I wandered to my couch. Jay, my husband came down the stairs. I confessed again to him. Each word felt like ice and lava at the same time...I held nothing back. He consoled me and reassured me as best as he could that we would be ok.

When we sat down for the nurse's call that night, I felt the tears start to fall before I could even say a word. I told her what I'd told the helpline nurse: "I don't feel safe. I feel like I'm dying." She listened. She didn't rush me, didn't try to fix me. She simply let me put words to the pain I'd been carrying for so long.

By the end of that session, I understood that what I was experiencing wasn't just stress or burnout. It was something deeper—major depressive disorder. The diagnosis was both terrifying and oddly liberating. For so long, I had blamed myself for not being able to "tough it out," for not being strong enough to thrive in an environment that demanded constant self-sacrifice. Now, I knew it wasn't just weakness; it was illness, and I was entitled to care.

That evening, I wrote in my journal for the first time in months. The words came in fits and starts, but they were honest: "I chose to ask for help. I don't know what comes next. But I can't go back to pretending." I wrote about how even with the world telling me I was "safe," my soul had known better—had screamed for freedom until I finally listened.

I texted Jhosh, my anchor through so much uncertainty: "I finally asked for help. I need this trip with you more than ever." His reply was immediate, as always: "I'm here. We'll get through this together."

That February day did not end with instant transformation. There was no magical moment when the pain disappeared. But it was the start of a different kind of journey—a messy, necessary, and ultimately redemptive process of unmasking. For the first time, I allowed myself to hope that healing was possible, that I was worthy of something more than survival.

I didn't know how I would move forward, but I knew one thing with absolute clarity: I had chosen myself. Not just in theory, but in action. That was enough to get me through the night, and into the first fragile steps of the next chapter.

Chapter 2: Wearing the Mask: Living for Others

Growing up in the humid, sun-drenched neighborhoods of Florida, I learned early that family could mean both comfort and isolation. Unlike many of my classmates, there were no aunts, uncles, or cousins gathering on weekends. My parents had left their hometowns and planted us in a new state, far from the extended family that might have offered backup, understanding, or even just someone else to shoulder the load. Our home was our entire world, and inside its walls, I became something I never really chose—the glue that tried to hold everyone together.

Ours was a house bursting with the energy and noise of four children. As the only girl sandwiched between three brothers, I occupied a unique and, at times, lonely role. My older brothers tested boundaries and claimed their independence as their right. My brothers, close in temperament, formed their own alliance—sometimes against the world, often against me. I was the girl in the middle, both literally and figuratively.

When I was still too young to fully understand, my parents began trusting me with the keys to the house. I became a latch key kid, responsible for letting myself in, starting homework, and making sure the chores were done. I swept floors, did laundry, and kept tabs on my brothers, all while trying to anticipate what my parents would want to see when they walked through the door: a clean house, homework finished, kids not fighting. I learned to read moods the way some kids learned to read maps—scanning faces for the weather of the evening and adjusting myself accordingly.

With no extended family to buffer the stress, my parents leaned on me in ways that felt normal at first but grew heavier over time. I became the peacekeeper, the one who intervened when tempers flared, who tried to keep the boys in line, who smoothed over my parents' worries with reassurances that everything was fine—even when it wasn't. I learned to be the "good kid," the one who followed the rules, made decent grades, and never caused trouble. At first, I thought this was what love looked like.

But my brothers saw things differently. To them, my rule-following and eager-to-please demeanor were a betrayal. I was the squeaky clean middle child, the girl who played by the book and, in their eyes, set an impossible standard. Their resentment simmered just beneath the surface, expressed in teasing, eye rolls, or outright exclusion. Sometimes they accused me of being the favorite, the one who made the rest of them look bad. I desperately wanted to belong to the wild brotherhood they shared, but more than that, I wanted peace—at home, at school, in my own heart.

So I doubled down on the mask. I became hyper-vigilant, always scanning for what needed to be done to keep everyone happy, to avoid conflict, to minimize the friction that seemed to erupt so easily among us. When my parents were stressed or tired, I'd quietly do more—taking on chores without being asked, biting my tongue when I wanted to argue, offering up my lunch money for pizza night or school supplies. I told myself that being good was the best way to be loved, and I clung to that belief as fiercely as a child clings to her favorite stuffed animal.

This way of being followed me out of childhood and into adolescence, layering itself into my personality until it felt inseparable from who I was. At school, I became the dependable friend, the one who remembered birthdays, lent out pencils, and quietly absorbed the drama of others without ever asking for help in return. Teachers praised my maturity; neighbors complimented my helpfulness. Each nod of approval reinforced my sense that keeping the peace—being easy, being good—was my role, my responsibility, my worth.

But inside, the cost was mounting. I envied kids who could slam doors, shout "it's not fair!" and demand attention for themselves. I wondered what it would feel like to be selfish, even for a moment. I noticed how my brothers, for all their chaos, seemed freer in their defiance than I ever felt in my obedience. I felt the loneliness of being the one who carried the load quietly, who never asked for more, who never admitted she was tired or hurt.

As I grew older, the mask only became heavier. My brothers' detachment solidified into distance. My parents, grateful for my reliability, leaned on me even more. And I, unsure of what else to do, kept trying to be "good"—even as the definition of "good" shifted and expanded with every new demand. I became the emotional caretaker, the one who noticed when someone was upset, who offered comfort and solutions, who tried to keep the family from splintering under the weight of unspoken tensions.

This role—the mask of the peacekeeper—became so automatic that I rarely questioned it. I was praised for my selflessness, my composure, and my ability to put others first. But I was also deeply, quietly resentful. I wanted someone to notice how hard I was trying, how much I was carrying. I wanted to be seen, not just as the good kid, but as a person with her own needs, her own aches and longings.

Looking back, I see how this early apprenticeship in people-pleasing shaped every relationship that followed. I carried the mask with me into adulthood, into work, into friendship, into love. I became the one who anticipated and solved problems, who kept the peace at all costs, who quietly accepted praise and internalized blame. The mask protected me from conflict but also from connection. It kept me safe but also kept me small.

The cost of living for others—of wearing the mask—was, ultimately, losing sight of myself. The mask promised belonging and safety, but delivered isolation and exhaustion. By the time that February morning arrived, the mask had become so tight I could barely breathe.

In the chapters that follow, I will share what it took to

finally start peeling it away. If you, too, have learned to be the peacekeeper, the good kid, the one who smooths the path for everyone else, I hope my story will remind you: you deserve to take up space, to have needs, to be loved—not for your role, but for your real, unmasked self.

Chapter 3:
The Illusion of Safety: The High Cost of "Success"

There's a certain kind of irony in being called "goals" when you feel like you're barely holding on. It was such a small moment, and yet, it was the pebble that finally started the avalanche. My cousin's best friend, Abbey, said it so casually, almost like a compliment: "You're goals. Seriously." I remember smiling and nodding, but inside, something twisted. I wanted to ask her if she knew how hollow that word sounded to someone who felt like a fraud in her own life.

From the outside, it did look like I had achieved everything a person was supposed to want. I had a corporate position at a Fortune 100 company, a steady yearly bonus, a pension plan—a husband, a step-kid, and a house on one of the most sought-after streets in town. Neighbors loved to describe our street as one of the last "Norman Rockwell neighborhoods," a place where kids rode bikes on tree-lined streets and the mailman still knew everyone by name. If someone had painted my life, it would have looked like the American Dream incarnate.

But the truth was, I had faked it till I made it. And somewhere along the way, I lost track of who I actually was, or what I truly wanted.

Abbey's comment stuck with me. That word—"goals"— echoed in my mind as I went through the motions of my daily life. I started to see the gap between what others perceived and what I actually felt. My confidence was crippled, drowning in a sea of grief and depression. I was still reeling from personal losses, still trying to find a way to carry my sadness without it ruining the lives of those around me. But I was also desperately trying to keep my career on track, to create some illusion of normalcy and balance when everything inside me felt brutal and raw.

The last few years at my job were the hardest. The company, like so many others, had mastered the art of the slow burn—pushing employees to do more with less, reassigning responsibilities, and shifting expectations without ever acknowledging the human cost. I was constantly told to "prove my worth," and yet, paradoxically, I was also told that what I was doing didn't warrant being "graded" any differently than anyone else. My work was good enough to fill the gaps, good enough to be relied upon, but not good enough to be recognized.

Looking back now, I see it for what it was: abuse. A toxic cycle that ground me down, lowered my standards, taught me to grit my teeth and pretend that being content with less was some sort of virtue. I didn't realize how much I had internalized this message until I found myself defending my own qualifications for a role I had practically built from scratch.

The final blow came during one of the hardest chapters of my personal life. I was deep in grief, but still, I was pushing myself to fill the gaps at work—taking on extra projects, seeing what the team needed, creating a job description for a role that I knew, in my bones, was essential. When the position finally opened, I did what seemed logical: I told my manager I wanted to apply. Her reaction was instant, almost comical in its cruelty.

She laughed. "Why would you think you're qualified for that role?"

I still remember the surge of humiliation, the sting of betrayal. My mind reeled, scrambling for words to justify myself. "I don't know why," I said, and heard my own voice tremble. "Maybe it's because I've been working on filling this gap and doing sprint projects for the past year and a half. I went back to school last year to gain knowledge for this very role." I tried to sound calm, but what came out was laughter—a strange, brittle sound that was half defense mechanism, half disbelief at how surreal the moment was. I laughed until I cried, the boundaries between the two feelings blurred by months of holding it all in.

She apologized, but the damage was done. I got off the phone and, for the first time in a long time, allowed myself to really feel the depth of my disappointment. That night, I sat down with my journal and wrote words I had never dared to say out loud: "I fire [name withheld] as my manager." It was a small act of rebellion, a private declaration that I was done handing over my worth to people who couldn't see it.

That was my breaking point. From that moment forward, I began to quietly quit—not in the way that makes headlines, but in the way that matters most. I stopped giving them the parts of me that I knew they would never value. I started to fade myself out, to conserve my energy for something else, something better—something that might, in time, help me rediscover who I actually was.

Corporate life had always been a tightrope walk, but by then, I knew the fall was inevitable. I was never going to fit in, not really—not in a culture that rewarded obedience and punished authenticity, that made you feel like an imposter no matter how hard you worked. The humiliation of that conversation, the realization that I didn't even like the person I had become in order to succeed there, was enough to finally set me free.

I felt betrayed—not just by my manager, but by a system I had spent years trying to please. I had spent so long convincing myself that if I just worked harder, followed more rules, kept the peace at home and at work, I would eventually feel like I belonged. But all I felt was empty, exhausted, and profoundly alone.

Looking back, I see that being labeled "goals" was never about me. It was about the story other people wanted to see. But stories can be rewritten, and masks can be removed. That realization, painful as it was, it was the first step toward finding my way back to myself.

Chapter 4: The Journey Begins: Healing on the Road

When I first landed in Italy, my body felt heavy, as if I had carried the entire weight of my unraveling life across the ocean with me. On paper, this was supposed to be the trip of a lifetime—a chance to see the world, to taste freedom, to fill my senses with art, food, and history. In reality, I was bone-tired. The exhaustion was more than jet lag; it was the accumulation of years spent in survival mode, pretending I was fine, pushing through grief, and holding myself together by force of will alone.

My first days in Rome blurred together in a haze of sleep and wakefulness. I slept most of the day, cocooned in the anonymous comfort of our apartment, letting my body sink into a rest it had been begging for. At night, when the city hummed with energy and life, I found myself wide awake. The streets outside were alive with voices, clinking glasses, and the distant echo of laughter. But inside, I was adrift—restless, my mind racing with everything I had left behind and everything I had yet to face.

In those sleepless hours, I began to draw again. I'd packed a small sketchbook, almost as an afterthought, but it became my anchor. I'd sit on the narrow balcony, listening to the mopeds whir past, and let my pen wander across the page. At first, my drawings were tentative—quiet lines and half-finished shapes, like the beginnings of a language I'd forgotten how to speak. But slowly, as the days passed, I started to fill the pages with the sights around me: the curve of a Roman arch, the silhouette of a cypress tree against a pink sunset, the swirl of a cappuccino in a delicate cup.

I found solace in aimless wandering. Rome is a city that invites you to get lost, to let go of maps and schedules and simply follow your curiosity. Most mornings, I'd wake up groggy, Jhosh would make me coffee, and then I would set out with no destination in mind, well maybe the gelato shop. The cobblestone streets twisted and turned, leading me past ancient ruins and hidden piazzas, sun-dappled courtyards and bustling markets. I let my feet carry me, trusting that wherever I ended up would be enough.

In those solitary walks, I began to reconnect with the parts of myself I had neglected for so long. I'd pause to watch artists at work on the Ponte Sant'Angelo, or listen to the lilt of Italian floating through the air as families gathered for lunch. Sometimes I'd sit quietly in a church, not for prayer, but for the hush and the coolness, the sense of being small but safe in a world much larger than my own pain.

Meditation became another lifeline. It wasn't the perfectly curated, Instagram-ready kind of practice—just me, sitting on the edge of my bed, closing my eyes, and focusing on my breath. At first, my mind was a riot of noise, replaying old wounds and future worries. But gradually, I learned to sit with the discomfort, to let the thoughts come and go without judgment. I was relearning how to be present, how to exist without needing to fix or achieve or prove anything.

Italy was the best place for me to rediscover my appetite— for food, yes, but also for life. In the weeks leading up to the trip, my hunger had vanished. Food tasted like cardboard, and eating felt like a chore. But here, surrounded by the warmth of Roman hospitality, I found myself drawn back to the table. I started small: a piece of crusty bread dipped in olive oil, a slice of ripe tomato, a forkful of pasta so simple and perfect it nearly made me weep. Each meal was a quiet act of rebellion against the numbness that had taken over my body. I let myself savor every bite, letting the pleasure of eating become a reminder that I was still alive, still worthy of care.

My most memorable meal was when a server saw me sopping up the leftover pasta sauce with bread. He said without hesitation, "now you're a Real Italian". My heart still fills with gratitude for being seen and able to connect with a stranger in that moment. I was present and had my appetite back.

Slowly, the rhythms of the city began to seep into me. Rome is a place where past and present coexist, where beauty and chaos mingle on every corner. I watched as locals lingered over coffee, as lovers strolled hand in hand along the Tiber, as children played soccer in the shadow of two-thousand-year-old ruins. Their ease was contagious, their joy a quiet invitation to let go of urgency and simply be.

I realized, in those meandering days, that what brought me joy was not achievement or approval, but connection—learning something new, sharing a smile, feeling the sun on my face. I remembered how much I loved learning, how curiosity had once been my constant companion. I let myself ask questions again, to delight in the unknown rather than fear it. I started to feel, in small moments, that life could be more than endurance. It could be enjoyed.

Some days were still hard. The grief and depression didn't magically disappear in the Roman sunlight. There were mornings when I woke up heavy with sadness, nights when loneliness pressed in. But for the first time in a long time, I felt the possibility of healing. I didn't have to be "goals" or even "okay." I just had to be here, now, in my own skin, finding small pockets of pleasure as I went.

Italy gave me the space to begin again. It reminded me that healing isn't something you achieve by force of will; it's something that happens in the quiet, in the in-between, in the simple acts of drawing, eating, walking, and breathing. I started to believe, just a little, that I could build a life not around what others expected of me, but around what truly brought me joy.

And so, with every step on those ancient stones, every meal shared, every page filled with ink, I began the slow, unsteady work of coming home to myself.

Chapter 5: Rediscovering My Body and Soul

The Eternal City has a way of humbling even the most restless of souls. As the days in Rome unfolded, I found myself lulled into a rhythm that was equal parts ancient and new: long afternoon naps, slow walks under blooming wisteria, evenings gazing at the golden glow of the city lights. My body, which had become so foreign to me in the months leading up to my departure, was slowly thawing, relearning pleasure and rest. Yet, despite the progress, grief and insomnia still clung to me like a second skin.

It was during one particularly restless night that the next great shift happened—one that would set the course for everything that followed. I remember it clearly: lying wide awake in my rented flat, Roman moonlight pooling on the floor, the sounds of the city filtering in through half-open windows. Sleep would not come, no matter how many times I tossed and turned, no matter how many deep breaths I took or how many times I tried to meditate my way back into my body.

Like most insomniacs of the modern age, I reached for my phone, scrolling through Instagram in the hope that a few moments of harmless distraction might finally lull me to sleep. Instead, I stumbled upon a video of Oprah Winfrey—her voice, warm and familiar, breaking through the haze of exhaustion.

She said, "Most people don't ever ask themselves what they truly want."

The words struck me like thunder. They reverberated in my chest, echoing louder than the cacophony of self-criticism and doubt that usually kept me company at night. Had I ever really asked myself that? Had I, Elaina, ever looked beyond the surface—beyond the expectations, the people-pleasing, the relentless striving—and simply asked, "What do I want?"

I set my phone aside and whispered the question into the

darkness, "Elaina, what do you want?"

The response from somewhere deep inside me was immediate and, honestly, a little absurd: "CAKE!"

I actually giggled out loud, startled by the honesty and irreverence of my own subconscious. Cake—of course. Who doesn't want cake? But as I sat with the word, I realized it wasn't just about dessert. There was something more, a curiosity bubbling up inside me.

There's got to be an acronym here, I thought. The word rolled around in my mind, and suddenly, the answer flowed out as if it had been waiting all along:

Connection. Authenticity. Kindness. Evolution.

That's what I want. That's what I've always wanted. It was so simple, so obvious, and yet I'd never given myself permission to name it. I want to connect, truly and deeply, with people and places and moments. I want to live authentically, to show up as myself—no masks, no apologies. I want to practice kindness, towards others but also towards myself, and I want to keep evolving, growing, learning, and becoming.

I want my life to be about **CAKE.**

For the first time in a long time, I felt a spark of joy. Not the fleeting, performative kind, but the real thing—joy that bubbles up from within and makes you want to laugh, cry, and dance all at once. I felt awake in a way that had nothing to do with insomnia and everything to do with remembering who I was when no one else was watching.

The next morning, I woke up with those words on my lips. I wrote them in my journal, doodled them in the margins of my sketchbook, and whispered them under my breath as I wandered through the city. CAKE became my mantra, my compass as I began to piece together a vision for my life that had nothing to do with corporate titles or external validation, and everything to do with how I wanted to feel—connected, authentic, kind, and ever-evolving.

As the days passed, I returned to my body, slowly and gently. I listened when it wanted to rest, honored when it wanted to move. I fed it with care, savoring each meal as both nourishment and celebration. I let myself be present in my own skin, to feel pleasure without guilt and pain without shame. I walked, drew, meditated, and watched the world unfold around me with the curiosity of a child and the hard-won wisdom of someone who knows what it is to break and begin again.

Rome, with its endless layers of history and possibility, became the backdrop for my rediscovery. It was here, beneath the shadow of ancient ruins and among the laughter of strangers, that I remembered what it meant to live for myself. To want, to hope, to dream—not for anyone else, but for me.

CAKE became my permission slip, my daily practice, my rebellion against a lifetime of self-denial. I let it guide me, one small choice at a time, as I began to rebuild my life from the inside out.

I didn't have all the answers, and I still don't. Healing is not a straight line, and there are days when the old wounds ache and the old fears whisper. But now, I have a question to return to whenever I lose my way: "Elaina, what do you want?" And I have an answer that feels true, sweet, and entirely my own.

I want CAKE. And every day, in small and ordinary ways, I am learning how to give it to myself.

Chapter 6: The Power of Friendship: Traveling with Jhosh

When I look back on my journey—the unraveling, the heartbreak, the slow and halting path toward healing—there is a thread of gold running through it all: my friendship with Jhosh. In a world that so often felt overwhelming and lonely, Jhosh was an anchor, a co-conspirator in joy, and, as it turns out, the very best travel companion I could have asked for as I tried to reclaim my life.

Traveling with a friend is a particular kind of intimacy. It's more than sharing hotel rooms and meals; it's sharing moods, silences, moments of awe and moments of exhaustion. When we initially planned the trip, we were both excited and nervous. A whole month to "Eat, Pray, Love" together. I wondered if my heaviness would weigh him down, or if the cracks in my composure would show more starkly in the daylight. I worried about being "too much"—too sad, too tired, too unlike the Elaina he was used to seeing.

But true friendship, I've learned, is elastic. It stretches to hold you, even when you are at your most uncertain.

The Language of Old Friends

From the moment we met up in Rome, it was clear that our friendship was a kind of homecoming. We settled into an easy rhythm—inside jokes, shared playlists, the shorthand of people who've spent years learning each other's quirks and tells. Jhosh didn't ask me to be anything but myself. He didn't rush me when I wanted to sleep in late, or wander aimlessly with no destination. He let the journey unfold, meeting me exactly where I was.

Some days, I was quiet and introspective, lost in my own thoughts as we navigated the narrow Roman streets. Other days, I felt lighter, buoyed by his laughter and the gentle, grounding presence he brought to the trip. On those mornings, we'd find a café and linger over coffee or smoothies, talking about everything and nothing. Jhosh had a way of making ordinary moments feel sacred.

Holding Space for Each Other

There's a particular kind of magic in traveling with a friend who knows how to hold space. Jhosh was present for me in ways that required no grand gestures—simply by listening, by not trying to fix what couldn't be fixed, by being patient with my uneven moods. He knew when to nudge me out of my shell and when to simply let me be.

One night, after a long day of sightseeing and people-watching at the Piazza Navona, we sat on a quiet bench eating gelato. The city glowed around us, ancient and alive, and for the first time in months, I felt a genuine sense of peace. I told him about my insomnia, about Oprah's words, about the CAKE mantra that had become my touchstone. He listened with the kind of attention that made me feel seen, not just heard.

"It's a good mantra," he said, smiling. "And you deserve every bit of it."

Just hearing that—having someone witness not just my pain, but my hope—was powerful in ways I'm not sure I'll ever be able to fully express. Friendship, I realized, is not just about having someone to share the good times with. It's about having someone who will stand by you as you rebuild, who will help you remember who you are when you've forgotten.

Adventures, Mishaps, and Laughter

Of course, traveling with Jhosh wasn't all deep conversations and emotional revelations. There was plenty of laughter, too. Like the time we got hopelessly lost in Trastevere, neither of us willing to admit we had no idea where we were going, or ordering from the "Too Good To Go" app, pizza, pastries, fruits and veggies, all in one night. We had too much food, but somehow it all got eaten.

We made up stories about the people we passed on the street, tried (and failed) to master the art of the Italian siesta, and took turns taking the worst tourist photos imaginable. Jhosh had a knack for finding the humor in any situation, and his lightness was contagious. Even on my hardest days, he could coax a genuine smile from me.

There is a freedom in being with someone who knows your history—the jokes that make you laugh, the stories that make you cry, the moments that have shaped you both. With Jhosh, I didn't have to explain why some days were harder than others. He understood without words, and that understanding was a balm.

Holding the Mirror

Good friends hold a mirror to us—not just reflecting back our wounds, but also our strengths, our joy, our capacity for growth. Jhosh reminded me of who I was beneath the grief and exhaustion. He celebrated my small victories, encouraged my curiosity, and gently challenged me when I slipped into old patterns of self-doubt.

When I talked about my career, my fears, my hopes for the future, he listened without judgment. He reminded me that my worth wasn't tied to a job title or a perfectly curated life. He helped me see that the life I wanted—the CAKE life—was not only possible, but already taking root.

The Gift of Shared Experience

Traveling with Jhosh in Italy became its own kind of therapy. There's healing in beauty, in adventure, in laughter—but there's a different kind of healing that comes from sharing those things with someone who truly knows you. Together, we built new memories, filled old wounds with light, and reminded each other of all the reasons life is worth savoring.

When it was time for us to return home, I felt a pang of sadness—but also a deep sense of gratitude. Our time together had been a gift, a reminder that even in the hardest seasons, we are not alone. Friendship, I realized, is not just about support; it's about celebration. It's about standing witness to each other's lives, and cheering each other on as we find our way forward.

Moving Forward, Together

As I continued my journey—through Italy, through healing, through rediscovering myself—I carried the lessons of our friendship with me. I carried his encouragement, his laughter, his unwavering belief in my ability to create a life rooted in connection, authenticity, kindness, and evolution.

The power of friendship is not in fixing what is broken, but in loving each other through the mess, in reminding each other of our wholeness, even when we can't see it ourselves. With Jhosh by my side, if only for a little while, I remembered how to be brave. I remembered how to hope.

And I remembered that, no matter where this path leads, the journey is sweeter—and lighter—when shared.

Chapter 7: Drawing Boundaries and Redefining Success

Returning home after Italy was almost as jarring as leaving in the first place. There's a peculiar shock to rediscovering your old life with new eyes, as if you're both an outsider and participant at once. The familiar routines—the kitchen counter cluttered with mail, the hum of street traffic outside my window—felt different, as if everything had shifted a few degrees. And, in a way, it had. I had.

Italy had taught me to listen—to my body, my intuition, my hunger (for food, for rest, for joy). It had given me room to breathe, to ask myself what I truly wanted, and to let the answer be something as simple and sweet as CAKE: Connection, Authenticity, Kindness, Evolution. But stepping back into my "real" life was a test: Would I revert to old habits, or could I build something new with these fragile, hard-won truths?

The Boundary Between Self and Expectation

For most of my life, boundaries were theoretical—a concept I admired but rarely practiced. I wanted to be liked, to be helpful, to be indispensable. I'd learned to stretch myself thin, to say yes when I meant no, to take pride in being the person others could count on. But the cost had been high: exhaustion, resentment, invisibility.

Italy had given me perspective, but now I needed practice. I made a list—small at first—of the areas in my life where I felt most depleted. Work was at the top. Even after my quiet quitting, the gravitational pull of over-responsibility was strong. I'd spent years defining my worth by my output, my promotion, my ability to fill in the gaps no one acknowledged. Now, I asked myself: What would it look like to draw a boundary here? What would it mean to protect my time, my energy, my spirit?

The answer was uncomfortable. It meant letting go of the illusion that I could control how others saw me. It meant submitting "good enough" work instead of perfect work, declining projects that didn't align with my values, and—most radical of all—not volunteering for more simply because I could. It meant being honest when my plate was full, and trusting that the world wouldn't fall apart if I stopped being the hero.

Boundaries with Family and Friends

If work was a battlefield, family and friends were a delicate dance. The roles we play in our relationships are often the hardest to change. I had always been the helper, the listener, the one who smoothed things over and made it all look easy. Now, I practiced saying, "I can't talk right now," or "I need some time alone." I let myself off the hook when I didn't have the capacity to show up for every event or solve every problem. Sometimes, I simply said no. Sometimes, I didn't explain.

Not everyone understood. Some people took offense, interpreting my new boundaries as distance or rejection. I had to remind myself—sometimes hourly—that boundaries are not walls. They are invitations: an invitation to meet me where I am, authentically, without pretense or resentment. And they are a promise to myself, a declaration that my needs matter, too.

Redefining What Success Means

Before my breakthrough, success was a finish line that always moved. It was the next promotion, the next gold star, the next box checked. It was being seen as "goals" from the outside, even as I felt empty inside. The more I achieved, the more hollow I became, until the mask itself began to suffocate me.

Now, I measure success differently. Was I living in alignment with my values? Was I honoring my body and my spirit? Was I making room for connection, authenticity, kindness, and evolution? These questions became my new compass.

Some days, success looked like a walk in the park, a slow meal, a conversation with a friend who truly saw me. Other days, it was finishing a project at home and leaving on time for appointments, without guilt. Some days, success meant letting myself cry when I needed to, rather than pushing the feeling away. It was quieter, gentler, and infinitely more sustainable than the old definition.

Rituals for Boundaries and Self-Respect

To make these changes stick, I created rituals—tiny ceremonies of self-respect. I scheduled "white space" into my calendar: blocks of time with nothing planned, reserved for rest or spontaneity. I set a timer at work to remind myself to take breaks, even if only for a glass of water or a stretch. I left my phone in another room when I needed to recharge.

And I wrote. I wrote letters to my future self, reminding her of what mattered. I wrote lists of things I could say no to, and things I genuinely wanted to say yes to. I wrote about what CAKE meant to me each day, and how I was honoring that choice, even in small ways.

The Backlash—and the Gifts

There were moments of backlash—internally and externally. Old habits die hard, and some days I slipped back into over-giving, over-explaining, overachieving. Some people in my world resisted the changes, missing the version of me that always said yes. But with every uncomfortable conversation, every pang of self-doubt, I reminded myself of why I started. I was not here to be everything to everyone. I was here to be fully, imperfectly myself.

The gifts of this practice became clear: more energy, more joy, more room for the things and people that mattered most. My relationships deepened, becoming more honest and mutually supportive. My work became more meaningful, as I focused on projects and tasks that aligned with my values. I felt lighter, freer, and more at home in my own skin.

Practicing progress not perfectionism with CAKE

Redefining success and drawing boundaries is not a one-time event. It's a daily, sometimes hourly, practice—a recalibration of what matters, a re-commitment to self-trust. The world may never applaud these private victories, but I do. Every day I choose CAKE—connection, authenticity, kindness, evolution—I am building a life that feels not only successful, but true.

I am still learning. I am still growing. But now, success is not a finish line. It is a way of being—a way of loving myself enough to say no, to say yes, and to live every day with intention.

And that, I am discovering, is the sweetest success of all.

Coming home from Italy, I was confronted by the daunting task of making sense of my old life with the new self that had emerged. The ancient streets of Rome and the gentle rhythms of daily pleasure had awakened a longing in me for change— but how, exactly, could I translate those revelations into the messy, interconnected world of home, work, and relationships? I knew something fundamental needed to shift, but I didn't know where to begin.

That's when I discovered Jay Shetty's life coach certification program. If you're not familiar, Jay Shetty is a former monk turned author and life coach whose work is rooted in both ancient wisdom and practical, actionable guidance for the modern world. The idea of learning from someone who had radically reinvented his own life, who had stripped everything down to the essentials and then rebuilt with intention, called to me. It sounded so much like what I was trying to do—only I was stumbling through it mostly alone.

Learning the Language of Boundaries

Enrolling in the Jay Shetty Certification School was more than a professional pivot; it was a lifeline. The curriculum was rigorous, yes, but it was also deeply personal. It asked me to look honestly at my own patterns: Where was I giving too much? Where was I holding back? What, truly, did I want to keep, and what was I ready to let go of?

Jay's teachings on boundaries were both simple and revolutionary: Boundaries are not about keeping people out, but about creating the conditions in which you can thrive. They are the invisible architecture of a life well-lived—a way to honor your needs, values, and energy so you can show up fully, both for yourself and others.

For the first time, I was invited to see boundaries not as selfish or cold, but as loving, necessary, and even sacred. I learned to identify the places where my boundaries were too porous—where I over-gave, over-extended, and lost myself trying to please others. I also recognized where my walls were too rigid, keeping out not just pain but also intimacy, support, and growth.

The Power of "Change, Modify, Delete"

One foundational tool I learned in the program was the practice of auditing my life with these three questions: What can be changed? What can be modified? What can be deleted? It became a gentle, nonjudgmental way to look at every area of my existence—work, relationships, habits, beliefs—and ask, "Does this fit who I am now? Does this fit the life I want to create?"

Change was about transformation: switching up routines, shifting roles, or finding new ways to approach old problems. Modifying was about subtle tweaks: adjusting expectations, renegotiating boundaries, or tweaking how much time and energy I gave to something. Delete, though, was the hardest— and the most freeing. It meant letting go of commitments, relationships, or even old parts of my identity that no longer served me.

I started small. I changed my morning routine to include journaling and meditation, making space for self-reflection before the world clamored for my attention. I modified my work boundaries, turning off email notifications after hours and giving myself permission to ask for help. I deleted obligations that drained me—social events I attended out of guilt, tasks I'd inherited without questioning, even certain relationships that were built on old versions of myself.

Practicing What I Preach

The irony of life coach training is that you can't help others unless you're willing to do the work yourself. As I practiced coaching peers in the program, I found myself identifying with their struggles: the fear of disappointing others, the discomfort of saying no, the guilt that came with prioritizing their own needs. Each practice session became a mirror, showing me how deeply ingrained my own people-pleasing patterns were.

But with every conversation, every boundary drawn, every "no" spoken with compassion, I grew stronger. I saw that boundaries were not barriers, but bridges—ways to connect more authentically, to show up with my whole self rather than a fractured, overextended version. I experienced firsthand what Jay often says: "You can't serve from an empty cup." Boundaries were how I started filling my own cup, drop by drop.

Redefining Success, Again

The deeper I went into the program, the more my definition of success evolved. No longer was it about external achievements or the approval of others. Success became about alignment—living in a way that was true to my values, my needs, my vision for my life. It was about showing up authentically, creating space for both rest and growth, and honoring my own evolution.

Now, when I measured my days, I didn't ask, "How much did I get done?" I asked, "Was I kind to myself? Did I honor my boundaries? Did I nurture connection, authenticity, kindness, and evolution—my CAKE mantra?" If the answer was yes, I was succeeding.

The Ripple Effect

As I grew more comfortable with boundaries, I noticed a ripple effect. My relationships deepened; conversations became more honest, less fraught with resentment or obligation. At work, I felt less anxious and more focused, able to give my best without burning out. In my coaching practice, I was able to hold space for others with empathy and clarity, modeling the very boundaries I hoped to inspire in my clients.

Of course, there were still moments of discomfort—old guilt, new resistance from others, the occasional slip into over-giving. But now I had tools, language, and a community of fellow coaches who understood the journey.

A Life That Fits

Learning to build boundaries that made sense for me wasn't just about keeping out what I didn't want; it was about creating space for what I did. Through the practice of change, modify, delete, and the wisdom of Jay Shetty's teachings, I began to reconstruct my life—piece by piece, choice by choice—into something that fit my new existence.

I am still learning, still evolving, but now I know: Boundaries are an act of love, both for myself and for those I care about. They are the foundation on which I am rebuilding, not just surviving, but thriving.

And for that, I am deeply, endlessly grateful.

Chapter 8: Building a Life of CAKE: Rituals and Daily Practices

If there's one thing Italy taught me—besides the joy of eating cake, literally and metaphorically—it's that the architecture of our days shapes the architecture of our lives. All the grand intentions, all the big dreams, all the boundary-setting in the world amount to little if I don't anchor them in daily practice. Ritual, I've come to realize, is the bridge between who I've been and who I'm becoming.

After so many years spent in survival mode, reacting to everything around me and putting myself last, I knew I had to create new rhythms. Rituals—intentional, repeated actions—became my way of reclaiming agency over my time, my energy, and my well-being. They gave me something to hold onto when the world felt chaotic, and a way to infuse each day with a sense of purpose and possibility.

The Morning Ritual: Nourishing, Medicate, Caffeinate, Meditate

My mornings used to be frantic, if I paid attention to them at all. I'd wake up already dreading the day ahead, skipping breakfast, checking emails before I'd even left my bed, and rushing into whatever crisis was waiting for me. No wonder I felt depleted before the sun had fully risen.

Italy changed that. There, life moved at a slower, more deliberate pace. People savored their coffee, greeted each other on the street, took time for breakfast. When I came home, I decided to try something radical: I would treat my mornings as sacred. I would begin each day by filling my own cup—literally and figuratively.

The first non-negotiable became breakfast. It sounds simple, but for someone who'd spent years ignoring her own hunger, it was a profound act of self-respect. Each morning, I made sure I ate—even if all I could manage was some fruit or toast. Feeding my body first thing became a way of saying, "You matter. You deserve care."

Then, I created my own quirky sequence: medicate, caffeinate, meditate. In that order.

- **Medicate**: As someone who needs daily medication, this step was both necessary and symbolic. It reminded me that self-care isn't optional, and that tending to my physical health is the foundation for everything else.

- **Caffeinate**: Coffee is more than a habit for me; it's a ritual. I took the time to make it just how I like it, often savoring the aroma and warmth as much as the taste. In those quiet minutes, I let myself wake up gently, sipping on possibility.

- **Meditate**: Even just ten minutes of meditation—sometimes less—made a world of difference. I would sit, eyes closed, focusing on my breath, letting my thoughts settle. Some days it felt transformative, other days it was just a pause before the busyness began. Either way, it was mine.

Over time, this sequence became both a shield and a launchpad. No matter what the day held, I had already claimed the first hour for myself. I had nourished my body, tended to my health, honored my mind. It set a tone of intentionality, making it easier to say yes to what served me, and no to what didn't, as the hours unfolded.

The Evening Routine: Reflect, Set Intentions, No Eating After 8 PM

If mornings are about preparation, evenings are about integration. I learned quickly that how I ended my day was just as important as how I began it. For years, my nights were chaotic—late-night snacking, mindless scrolling, replaying every mistake or worry as I tried to drift off to sleep.

That changed as I began to prioritize ritual over routine. My evenings became my time for reflection, intention, and gentle boundaries.

- **Reflect:** Before bed, I carve out a few minutes to look back at the day. Sometimes I journal, sometimes I simply sit in silence and ask myself what went well, what challenged me, and what I learned. This reflection is not about judgment, but about witnessing my own growth, day by day.

- **Set Intentions:** I jot down intentions for tomorrow—not a to-do list, but a to-be list. How do I want to show up? What qualities do I want to embody? Connection, authenticity, kindness, evolution—these are the touchstones I return to, again and again.

- **No Eating After 8 PM:** This boundary, strangely, became one of my favorites. I realized that late-night eating was often about numbing out rather than nourishing myself. By making 8 PM my cutoff, I reclaimed my evenings as a time for rest, not consumption. It was hard at first, but soon I found that my sleep improved, my body felt lighter, and I was more in tune with my true needs.

Ritual as Self-Respect

These daily practices are not about perfection. There are days when I forget, when I break my own rules, when life throws a curve ball and I have to adapt. But they are always there, waiting for me to return. Like stepping stones across a river, they help me cross from one day to the next with a sense of steadiness.

More than anything, my rituals are reminders: I am worthy of care. I am the architect of my experience. I get to choose, moment by moment, what I give my time and attention to. These choices, small as they seem, become the foundation of a life that feels both intentional and alive.

Living My CAKE mantra, One Day at a Time

Building a life of CAKE—connection, authenticity, kindness, evolution—is not a one-time event, but a daily practice. Each morning and evening, through these simple rituals, I recommit to the life I want: one where I am present, nourished, awake to the possibilities of each day.

My rituals are how I make room for joy, for learning, for softness and strength. They are how I remind myself that I am not just surviving, but choosing—again and again—to build a life that fits who I am now.

And that, I've learned, is the sweetest kind of cake there is.

Chapter 9: Embracing the Unknown: Trusting the Process of Change

There's a peculiar kind of fear that comes with letting go of the life you've always known, even when that life no longer fits. For so long, I clung to routine and predictability because they gave me the illusion of control. My calendar was packed, my goals were clear, and my days—though exhausting—felt safe in their familiarity. But when everything unraveled, when I broke under the weight of grief and burnout, I found myself in the vast, uncharted territory of the unknown.

At first, the uncertainty was terrifying. Every morning, I woke up with a sense that the ground beneath me was shifting. The old markers of success and security—job titles, praise, a tightly scheduled day—had lost their meaning. Without them, I didn't quite know who I was or where I was headed.

Italy was my first taste of freedom, but it was also my first confrontation with uncertainty. Each day was unscripted. Would I feel up to exploring, or would I retreat to my hotel and sleep? Would I connect with new people, or would I spend the day in quiet solitude? Would I find meaning, or just more questions? The only certainty was that I didn't know.

What surprised me was how, over time, the unknown became less threatening and more inviting. I started to see that there was a kind of magic in not knowing. Without a rigid plan, I was free to follow my curiosity. I found hidden courtyards and unexpected conversations. I allowed myself to wander without a map—sometimes literally, sometimes metaphorically. I discovered that uncertainty, rather than being a void to fear, could be a space for possibility.

The Stories We Tell Ourselves

One of the biggest lessons of this chapter of my journey was learning to listen to the stories I told myself about change. For years, I'd internalized the idea that good things only come to those who plan, prepare, and control every variable. Uncertainty, I believed, was to be avoided at all costs.

But as I faced the unknown—first in Italy, then back home—I realized that story was rooted in fear, not truth. Life is inherently uncertain. Plans fall apart, people change, dreams evolve. The more I tried to force certainty, the more anxious and rigid I became. The more I allowed for uncertainty, the more room I had for growth, creativity, and joy.

Trusting the process of change meant rewriting my inner narrative. Instead of asking, "What if everything goes wrong?" I started to ask, "What if something amazing happens?" Instead of demanding answers, I learned to sit with questions. Instead of bracing for disappointment, I opened myself to surprise.

The Practice of Surrender

Surrender is not a word I would have chosen for myself in the past. It sounded passive and weak. But I've come to understand it as an act of profound strength. Surrender, in this context, means accepting that I cannot control every outcome. It means letting go of the belief that I have to have everything figured out before I can move forward.

In practice, surrender looked like this: trusting that I could figure things out as I went, rather than needing all the answers in advance. Allowing myself to take imperfect action, to make mistakes, to learn along the way. It meant forgiving myself when things didn't go according to plan, and being gentle with myself in moments of doubt.

Surrender also meant embracing help and guidance. During my life coach training, I learned to lean on my mentors and peers, to ask for support when I needed it. I let go of the idea that I had to be the expert or the hero all the time. I became a student again—curious, open, willing to be changed by what I didn't know.

Rituals for Navigating Uncertainty

Of course, embracing the unknown didn't mean giving up all structure. My morning and evening rituals became even more important during times of change. They were the touchstones that kept me grounded, even when everything around me felt up in the air. By anchoring my days with intention and care, I created a sense of safety within myself, no matter what was happening outside.

I also developed a practice of "checking in" with myself throughout the day. I would pause, take a breath, and ask: "What do I need right now? What is mine to control, and what isn't?" These questions helped me release the urge to micromanage the future and return to the present moment.

The Gifts of the Unknown

Looking back, I see that the unknown gifted me things certainty never could. It gave me resilience—the knowledge that I can adapt, pivot, and thrive even in uncertainty. It gave me creativity—the freedom to try new things, to experiment, to play. It gave me humility—the reminder that I don't have all the answers, and that's okay.

Most of all, the unknown gave me faith. Not faith that everything would be easy or work out exactly as I hoped, but faith in myself. Faith that I could handle whatever came, that I could find meaning and beauty in the unfolding story of my life. Faith that even in the dark, there is always a next step, a next breath, a next possibility.

Trusting the Process

Trusting the process of change is an act of courage. It means stepping forward, even when the path isn't clear. It means letting go of who I thought I had to be, and making room for who I might become. It means believing that life is not a problem to be solved, but an adventure to be lived.

As I continue to rebuild my life, I remind myself daily: The unknown is not my enemy. It is the space where transformation happens. It is the field where CAKE—connection, authenticity, kindness, evolution—can truly take root.

And so, I walk forward, not with certainty, but with trust. Trust in the process. Trust in myself. Trust in the unfolding.

Chapter 10: The Art of Self-Compassion: Healing the Inner Critic

One of the most profound—and unexpected—turning points in my healing journey was learning to befriend my own mind. I used to believe that progress meant silencing my doubts, erasing my insecurities, and banishing the negative self-talk that so often accompanied me through each day. But the truth is, our inner critics are persistent; they don't disappear just because we wish them away. They linger in the background, whispering judgments and fears, especially when we're on the verge of change.

For years, my inner critic was a constant companion, but also a mysterious adversary. She was the voice that told me I wasn't good enough, that my dreams were foolish, that I should play it safe or try harder or be someone else entirely. She was relentless, and I never questioned her authority. It wasn't until I began my work as a life coach—learning to observe my thoughts with curiosity rather than judgment—that I realized: If I could name this voice, I could begin to change my relationship with her.

So, I named her **Evelyn**.

The act of naming my inner critic was quietly revolutionary. Suddenly, she became a character in my story rather than the unseen puppeteer. Evelyn was sharp, discerning, and often—if I'm honest—a little dramatic. She worried incessantly about what others thought, about failing, about missing out or messing up. She compared, she catastrophized, she clung to perfectionism like a life raft. But she also had a purpose: Evelyn wanted to keep me safe. Her methods were misguided, but her intentions, I realized, were rooted in protection.

Meeting Evie: My Inner Bestie

As I continued my self-compassion practice, I noticed another, subtler voice within me—a gentle counterpoint to Evelyn's criticism. This voice was kind, playful, and fiercely supportive. She cheered for my wins, comforted me in my lows, and approached my mistakes with a sense of curiosity rather than condemnation. She was the friend I'd always wanted, and the friend I needed to be to myself.

I named this voice **Evie.**

Evie was my inner bestie, the embodiment of self-compassion and encouragement. While Evelyn focused on what could go wrong, Evie reminded me of my strengths, my progress, and my inherent worthiness. She didn't ignore my fears, but she helped me see them in context. She didn't sugarcoat the truth, but she delivered it with warmth and hope.

The Dialogue Within

Naming Evelyn and Evie gave me the power to observe my inner dialogue rather than being swept away by it. When I caught Evelyn judging or shaming me—"You're not doing enough," "Why bother?"—I could pause, acknowledge her presence, and invite Evie into the conversation.

Sometimes, I imagined them sitting on opposite sides of a cozy table in my mind, having a debate about my latest decision or struggle. Evelyn would present her case—pointing out risks, recalling past failures, warning about disappointment. Evie would listen, then gently ask, "Is that the whole story? What else could be true? How can we approach this with kindness and curiosity?"

This ongoing dialogue helped me see that my thoughts were not facts—they were stories, shaped by my experiences, fears, and hopes. By balancing Evelyn's vigilance with Evie's compassion, I could make room for nuance and possibility.

Compassion and Curiosity: The Keys to Healing

The real transformation came when I stopped trying to silence Evelyn and instead chose to listen to her with compassion. Rather than arguing with her or trying to banish her, I learned to thank her for her concern. "Thank you, Evelyn, for wanting to protect me. I know you're scared. But I've got this. Let's check in with Evie and see what she thinks."

Evie, in turn, taught me the power of curiosity. When I felt anxious or ashamed, she encouraged me to ask, "What's really going on here? What do I need right now? How can I be gentle with myself in this moment?" Curiosity softened my judgments, opening a space for understanding and growth.

Instead of berating myself for feeling afraid or uncertain, I began to ask what those feelings were trying to tell me. Sometimes, they signaled a real need—rest, reassurance, support. Other times, they were echoes of old wounds, surfacing so they could be healed.

Practices for Befriending Your Inner Critics

This work is ongoing, but I've found a few practices that help me nurture my relationship with both Evelyn and Evie:

1. **Journaling the Dialogue:** When I'm stuck in self-criticism, I write out a conversation between Evelyn and Evie. Seeing their words on the page helps me separate their voices and recognize the wisdom in both caution and compassion.

2. **Self-Compassion Breaks:** Whenever Evelyn gets loud, I pause and place a hand on my heart. I tell myself, "This is a moment of suffering. Suffering is part of being human. May I be kind to myself right now." This simple act invites Evie's presence.

3. **Fact-Checking with Kindness:** I challenge Evelyn's harshest statements by asking, "Is this absolutely true? What would Evie say about this?" Often, the truth is more balanced and generous than my initial thoughts.

4. **Celebrating Small Wins:** Evie loves to celebrate. Whether it's getting out of bed on a hard day or setting a healthy boundary, I let her throw a little party in my mind. This reinforces self-compassion and builds confidence.

Integration: Living with Both Voices

Healing the inner critic isn't about erasing her—it's about integrating her. Evelyn will always have a seat at my table, but she no longer runs the show. Evie is there too, offering balance, perspective, and unconditional support.

This inner partnership has changed how I approach challenges, setbacks, and even success. When I stumble, Evelyn may grumble, but Evie reminds me that growth is rarely linear. When I achieve something meaningful, Evelyn might discount it, but Evie urges me to savor the moment.

Most importantly, this practice has taught me that self-compassion is not weakness—it is strength. It is the foundation of resilience, creativity, and authentic connection. By honoring both my fears and my hopes, I can meet myself exactly where I am, and move forward with courage and grace.

The Ongoing Journey

Some days, Evelyn is louder. Other days, Evie leads the way. But every day, I am learning to listen to both with an open heart. I am learning to see my thoughts not as facts, but as guides—inviting me to balance vigilance with kindness, caution with curiosity.

This is the art of self-compassion. It is the practice of loving myself through the mess, the magic, and the mystery of becoming. It is the foundation on which I continue to build a life of CAKE—connection, authenticity, kindness, evolution—one gentle step at a time.

Chapter 11: Finding Joy in Small Things: Reclaiming Play and Wonder

There's an old saying that joy is found in the journey, not the destination. For years, that sentiment felt like a distant ideal—something for people who didn't have to worry about deadlines, heartbreak, or the daily grind. My eyes had become attuned to what was urgent, what was lacking, what needed to be fixed or achieved. I rarely paused to notice the quiet miracles blooming all around me.

But as I began healing—through rituals, boundaries, self-compassion, and all those honest conversations with Evelyn and Evie—I realized how much I'd been missing. My world had become small, but not in the way that brings comfort or focus. It was small in the way of grayness, of forgetting how to look up, of losing touch with the playful, curious parts of myself.

Italy, in its slow magic, began to chip away at that numbness. I watched old men play cards in the park with the intensity of championship athletes. I lingered over gelato, letting each flavor melt into sweetness. I wandered ancient streets, letting myself get lost just to see what I might find. The wonder of new places, new tastes, and new rhythms reminded me what it felt like to be alive and alert—to be a person capable of delight.

The Practice of Noticing

When I returned home, I made a quiet vow: to notice, every day, at least one thing that brought me joy. Not the grand gestures or milestone achievements, but the fleeting, ordinary moments. The way sunlight poured through the kitchen window. The first sip of coffee in the morning. The sound of rain tapping on the roof. The familiar weight of my favorite book in my hands.

At first, it felt forced, a little silly even. I'd been conditioned to believe that joy should be earned, that it was the reward for hard work or overcoming adversity. But slowly, the practice of noticing became natural. My mind, ever prone to worry, began to make room for wonder. I found myself smiling at strangers, marveling at the resilience of weeds pushing through concrete, laughing at the antics of squirrels on the fence.

This practice wasn't just about gratitude, though that was part of it. It was about remembering that play and wonder aren't childish—they're essential. They root us in the present, soften our edges, and remind us that life is more than a list of obligations.

Giving Myself Permission to Play

One of the hardest (and most liberating) realizations was that I needed to give myself permission to play. As an adult, especially one who'd worn the armor of "responsible achiever" for so long, play felt frivolous. But I began to see how essential it was for my healing. Play was how I reconnected with my intuition, my creativity, and even my body.

Sometimes, play looked like dancing around my living room to 90s pop songs, singing off-key and laughing at myself. Other times, it was trying a new recipe, making a glorious mess in the kitchen, and not caring if it turned out "perfect." I started doodling in the margins of my journal, letting lines and shapes emerge without judgment. I bought a puzzle and lost track of time fitting the pieces together. I let myself be a beginner again.

It wasn't always easy. Evelyn, my inner critic, would often chime in: "Shouldn't you be doing something more productive?" But Evie, my inner bestie, countered with gentle encouragement: "You deserve this. Joy is productive. Play is how you return to yourself."

The Wonder of Nature and the World

Spending time in nature became another source of wonder. I began taking slow walks in the park, not for exercise or to check off a fitness goal, but to simply be. I watched clouds shift shapes, listened to birdsong, and let my hands trail through tall grass. Sometimes, I picked wildflowers, pressing them between the pages of my journal as tiny reminders to keep looking for beauty.

Nature taught me about patience and presence. I saw how seasons change without hurry, how flowers bloom and fade in their own time. I realized that I, too, was allowed to move at my own pace, to trust the unfolding of my own life.

Curiosity as a Pathway to Joy

Curiosity became my compass. Instead of asking, "What should I do?" I began to ask, "What's interesting here? What haven't I noticed before?" This shift opened up a thousand small adventures—trying a new route home, tasting an unfamiliar fruit, reading a book from a genre I'd never considered.

Curiosity also helped me approach difficult days with gentleness. Instead of berating myself for feeling low, I'd ask, "What might help right now? What small comfort or pleasure can I offer myself?" Sometimes the answer was as simple as a hot bath, a favorite song, or a call to a friend.

Sharing Joy With Others

As I reclaimed joy for myself, I found it naturally spilling over into my relationships. I started sending spontaneous texts to friends describing little joys—a beautiful sky, a funny encounter, a delicious meal. I invited people to join me for walks, movie nights, or creative projects, not out of obligation, but out of genuine excitement to share the experience.

The more I shared, the more I realized: joy is contagious. It grows in the giving and receiving, in the shared laughter and collective awe. Even on hard days, knowing I could bring a smile to someone else's face made my own light burn brighter.

Joy as Resistance and Renewal

In a world that often glorifies busyness and struggle,

choosing joy is an act of resistance. It's a refusal to let pain or pressure define the limits of my experience. It's a commitment to savoring life, even in the midst of uncertainty.

Reclaiming play and wonder hasn't erased my challenges, but it has changed how I meet them. Joy is now a resource, a well I can draw from when I'm weary or discouraged. It reminds me that I am more than what I produce or achieve—I am a living, feeling, curious being, worthy of delight.

The Everyday Miracle

If healing has a sound, it's laughter bubbling up unexpectedly, or the quiet gasp of awe at a sunset. If healing has a taste, it's the first bite of cake, savored slowly. If healing has a look, it's the softening of my own eyes in the mirror, recognizing the woman who has learned to see the world—and herself—with wonder again.

This is how I measure progress now: not just in milestones, but in moments. Not just in what I accomplish, but in how often I allow myself to play, to marvel, to feel joy for no reason at all.

And in this way, I am learning to live my one precious life— not someday, but right now—one small, joyful thing at a time.

Chapter 12: Building Community:
The Power of Vulnerable Connection

When I first began to rebuild my life after Italy, I thought a lot about boundaries, self-care, and the importance of solitude. But as the weeks passed and the seasons turned, I realized that healing—and thriving—also required something I'd long neglected: true connection. Not just the surface-level hellos or the polite, distant smiles exchanged with acquaintances, but real, vulnerable connection that grounds us in a sense of belonging.

Ironically, I didn't start this part of my journey for myself. I started it for Lucy.

Lucy: The Four-Legged Ambassador

Lucy, my King Charles Cavalier, is the living embodiment of joy and beauty. With her silky ears, soulful brown eyes, and that constantly wagging tail, she radiates a warmth that is impossible to resist. She greets every day—and every person— with the open-hearted enthusiasm of someone who has never known a bad moment. Walking her is a lesson in presence, in savoring the smallest pleasures. But more than that, Lucy is an ambassador of connection.

When I first moved into my neighborhood, I kept to myself. I was still raw from my own losses and transitions, unsure how much of myself I wanted to share with others. But Lucy had other plans. From day one, she insisted on meeting everyone. She would pull me toward new faces, her whole body quivering with excitement at the prospect of a new friend.

It wasn't long before I realized that Lucy was not just walking me around the block—she was walking me straight into a new chapter of community.

Meeting My Neighbors—One Wag at a Time

It started with small moments. As we strolled down the

sidewalk, Lucy would spot a neighbor tending their garden or unloading groceries and trot right over, tail wagging furiously. "She's so beautiful!" they'd exclaim, bending down to scratch her behind the ears. "What's her name?" That single question opened the door to conversation.

At first, the exchanges were brief and practical. "She's Lucy," I'd say, smiling shyly. "She loves meeting new people." But Lucy's unguarded joy was contagious. People lingered a little longer, asked about her breed, shared stories about their own pets. Sometimes, Lucy would insist on sitting at someone's feet until they laughed and knelt down to greet her properly.

Before long, we weren't just exchanging names; we were sharing bits of our lives. One neighbor told me about her recent retirement. Another confessed he was new to the area and didn't know anyone yet. A teenager down the block gushed about his dream of becoming a veterinarian. A woman a few houses away invited me to sit on her porch with Lucy play with her dog Scrappy.

Lucy, in her gentle, persistent way, had become a bridge. Through her, I was learning to say yes to connection, even when it felt vulnerable or uncertain.

The Gift of Everyday Encounters

There's something beautifully disarming about meeting through the eyes of a dog. Lucy didn't care about anyone's job title, appearance, or past mistakes. She cared only about the present moment—the possibility of play, affection, or a new scent to discover. Her openness gave me permission to let my own guard down.

Some days, our walks became spontaneous social hours, as Lucy stopped to greet her "regulars." We'd talk about the weather, neighborhood news, or the best local restaurants. Other days, I found myself sharing more—about my journey, my struggles, and even my dreams. People responded in kind, offering encouragement, empathy, or simply a listening ear.

These small, daily encounters accumulated into something much larger—a sense of belonging that I hadn't realized I was missing. I began to look forward to seeing familiar faces, to checking in on neighbors and being checked in on in return. My neighborhood, once a collection of houses, became a community.

Vulnerability as the Gateway to Belonging

What surprised me most was how these connections deepened when I allowed myself to be vulnerable. Lucy was a natural icebreaker, but it was my willingness to share honestly that transformed acquaintances into friends. When a neighbor asked how I was doing, I stopped giving the automatic "Fine, thanks." Instead, I'd say, "It's been a hard week, actually. But Lucy's walks help." More often than not, this honesty was met with nods of understanding and their own stories of struggle or resilience.

I realized that community isn't built on perfection or small talk—it's built on the willingness to be seen and to see others in return. Lucy, with her unabashed affection, modeled this every day. She didn't hold back her joy or her disappointment; she lived fully in each moment, trusting that connection was always possible.

Creating Rituals of Togetherness

Inspired by these new bonds, I began to create small rituals of togetherness. neighbors would invite us to hang out in their backyard while our dogs played. Every morning we would greet our neighbors before they head

These gestures, simple as they were, made our little corner of the world feel warmer, safer, more alive. They reminded me that healing isn't just an individual journey; it's something we do together, in conversation and companionship.

The Unexpected Beauty of Community

Looking back, I am astonished by how much joy and meaning

Lucy has brought into my life—not just as my companion, but as my guide into community. Her presence opened doors I never would have knocked on. She taught me that sometimes, the path to belonging is as simple as showing up, wagging your tail, and saying hello.

In a world that often encourages isolation or surface-level interaction, Lucy's infectious joy reminds me that we are wired for connection. We are meant to share our lives, our struggles, our celebrations, and even our quiet moments of contentment. We are meant to belong.

And so, as I continue to walk these neighborhood streets with Lucy by my side, I carry her lessons with me: Approach each day—and each person—with curiosity and kindness. Don't be afraid to reach out, to linger, to share a piece of your heart. Community is built not in grand gestures, but in the accumulation of small, vulnerable moments, repeated again and again.

Lucy, with her boundless love, has shown me the way.

Chapter 13: Letting Go of Perfection: Embracing Messy Progress

If there's one lesson I've resisted more fiercely than any other on this journey, it's the imperative to let go of perfection. For much of my life, perfectionism felt not just like a personal standard, but a survival strategy. If I could get everything just right—my work, my appearance, my relationships—maybe I could avoid criticism, disappointment, or pain. Maybe I could finally earn the approval I craved, both from others and from myself.

Of course, perfection is a moving target. The more I chased it, the further it seemed to recede. When I did achieve something "perfect"—a glowing review at work, a meticulously planned event, a spotless home—I felt relief, but never real joy. There was always another thing to fix, another flaw to hide. The price of perfection was constant anxiety, exhaustion, and an ever-deepening disconnect from my authentic self.

Italy, with its ancient, crumbling beauty, began to shift my perspective. There, I saw centuries-old statues missing noses, frescoes faded by time, streets cobbled unevenly but still alive with laughter and music. Life was messy, imperfect—and utterly enchanting. I started to wonder: what if my own life didn't need to be perfect to be beautiful? What if, in fact, its imperfections were part of its unique charm?

Naming the Perfectionist Within

As I delved deeper into my self-compassion work, I realized that my inner critic, Evelyn, often wore the mask of perfectionism. She whispered that mistakes were unacceptable, that vulnerability was weakness, that only flawlessness was worthy of love. For years, I'd listened to her unquestioningly, believing that any slip-up would bring disaster.

But as I got to know Evie, my inner bestie, I started to hear another message: "You are enough, right now, exactly as you are." Evie encouraged me to see mistakes as evidence of courage, not failure. She reminded me that growth is rarely linear, and that every stumble is part of the dance.

The Courage to Be Messy

Letting go of perfection didn't happen all at once. It was a process of gentle, repeated practice—of choosing progress over perfection, again and again. I started by giving myself permission to do things badly, just for the experience of doing them.

If I tried a new recipe and it flopped, I laughed and ordered takeout. If I skipped a morning meditation, I forgave myself and tried again the next day. If I said the wrong thing in a conversation, I apologized and moved forward, trusting that relationships could survive a little awkwardness.

This willingness to be messy was liberating. I discovered that the world didn't end when I made a mistake. People didn't abandon me when I showed my flaws—in fact, they often felt closer to me. My own self-respect grew as I learned to honor effort and intention over results.

Messy Progress in Coaching and Community

My work as a life coach became a laboratory for embracing imperfection. Early on, I worried about saying the wrong thing or not having all the answers for my clients. But the more I allowed myself to be human—to admit what I didn't know, to be present rather than perfect—the deeper my connections became.

Clients responded to my authenticity, not my expertise. They felt seen and accepted, not judged. Together, we celebrated small wins, learned from setbacks, and laughed at our shared humanity. It turned out that my messiness was a gift, not a liability.

The same was true in my neighborhood community. When I dropped a plate of cookies on a neighbor's porch (literally— Lucy got excited and I lost my grip), I felt mortified. But my neighbor simply laughed, invited me in, and we ate the slightly smooshed cookies together. That imperfect moment became a cherished memory.

The Power of "Good Enough"

One of the most powerful shifts was redefining what "good enough" meant for me. Instead of seeing it as settling, I began to see it as sanity. Good enough meant I was present for my life, not just performing for an invisible audience. Good enough meant I could rest, play, and connect without the pressure to always be more.

This was not an excuse for carelessness, but an invitation to compassion. I still cared deeply about my work, my relationships, and my dreams—but I no longer demanded flawlessness as the price of admission.

Rituals for Embracing Messy Progress

- Celebrate Imperfect Wins: At the end of each week, I made a list of things I tried, regardless of outcome. Learning to salsa dance, hosting a book club, finishing a painting—even if they were messy, they were victories.

- **Practice Self-Forgiveness:** When I caught myself spiraling into self-criticism, I paused and placed a hand on my heart. "I am human. I am learning. I forgive myself."

- **Share the Mess:** I made a habit of telling friends and clients about my own foibles and failures. The more I shared, the more others did too. Vulnerability became a source of connection, not shame.

- **Let Go of All-or-Nothing Thinking**: If I couldn't do a full workout, I did five minutes of stretching. If I couldn't write a whole chapter, I wrote a single page. Progress, not perfection.

The Beauty of Becoming

In letting go of perfection, I rediscovered the beauty of becoming. Life is not a finished product; it's a work in progress, a collage of moments—some polished, some rough-edged, all uniquely mine. My worth is not tied to performance, but to presence. My value is not measured in flawlessness, but in the willingness to keep showing up, keep trying, keep loving.

The more I embraced this truth, the more alive I felt. I laughed more, took more risks, and found joy in the process rather than just the result. I saw that the cracks in my life let the light in. That my imperfections made me real, relatable, and resilient.

So here's to the mess. Here's to the courage to be seen in all our imperfect glory. Here's to progress, not perfection—and to the sweet, surprising freedom it brings.

Chapter 14: Living the CAKE Mantra: Integrating Connection, Authenticity, Kindness, and Evolution

As the threads of my journey began to weave into something resembling a new life, I found myself returning again and again to the four words that had quietly emerged as my guiding stars: **Connection, Authenticity, Kindness, Evolution**. CAKE. The CAKE mantra started as a small touchstone—an acronym scribbled in my journal, a whispered reminder on tough days—but over time, it grew into a philosophy for living. It became the foundation for how I chose to show up for myself and for the world around me.

Discovering the Ingredients

Much like baking a real cake, I learned that living the CAKE mantra wasn't about perfection or following a strict recipe. It was about bringing together the best ingredients I had—every day, in every moment—and trusting that the result would be nourishing, even if it didn't always look like I expected.

- **Connection** meant saying yes to the people and places that made me feel alive. It was the laughter shared with neighbors over Lucy's antics, the deep conversations with coaching clients, the quiet moments of presence with myself. Connection reminded me that I didn't have to do life alone.

- **Authenticity** asked me to drop the mask, to speak my truth, and to honor my feelings—even when they were messy or inconvenient. It was the voice of Evie, my inner bestie, gently reminding me that who I am is enough. Authenticity freed me from the prison of perfection, allowing me to live from the inside out.

- **Kindness** was the soft glue that held it all together. It was the way I spoke to myself when Evelyn, my inner critic, got loud. It was the extra loaf of banana bread for a neighbor, the handwritten note, the smile to a stranger on a hard day. Kindness was how I learned to move through the world—with compassion, curiosity, and an open heart.

- **Evolution** was the promise that I didn't have to stay stuck. It was the willingness to grow, to try new things, to let go of what no longer served me. Evolution was the daily practice of asking, "What's the next right step?" and trusting that change, however small, was a sign of life.

Bringing CAKE Into Daily Life

As I grew more intentional about living these values, I found that they naturally intertwined with the rhythms and rituals I'd established. My morning routine—eat, medicate, caffeinate, meditate—became an act of kindness and authenticity, honoring my needs and setting the tone for the day. Evening reflection and intention-setting helped me stay connected to myself and my goals, while my commitment to not eating after 8 PM reinforced healthy boundaries and self-respect.

Lucy, my joyful canine companion, was my daily reminder to seek connection—in the wag of her tail, the warmth of her greeting, the way she drew me out of my shell and into the world. Through her, I learned that connection could be simple, spontaneous, and deeply rewarding.

Coaching brought CAKE to life in new ways. In every session, I strove to create a space where clients felt seen, heard, and valued. I celebrated their wins, honored their struggles, and encouraged them to approach their own lives with kindness and curiosity. Watching others grow and evolve became one of my greatest joys.

The Challenges of Integration

Of course, living the CAKE mantra isn't always easy. There are days when I feel disconnected, when authenticity feels risky, when kindness is reserved for everyone but myself, when evolution feels like two steps back for every one step forward. On those days, I return to the basics: breathe, notice, forgive, begin again.

I've learned that integration is a practice, not a destination. It's about bringing these values into the small, everyday moments: choosing to call a friend when I feel lonely, telling the truth about my feelings, offering myself grace when I fall short, taking a new class or reading a new book just because I'm curious. It's about living in alignment with what matters most, even when it's hard.

Living the CAKE mantra has had a ripple effect I never could have imagined. My relationships have deepened, my sense of purpose has expanded, and my resilience has grown. I'm no longer waiting for the "perfect" moment to start living my life; I'm finding meaning and joy in the here and now.

Even more, I've seen how my commitment to CAKE inspires others. Friends, neighbors, clients—they notice the shift. They ask about my routines, my coaching, my journey. Sometimes, they even adopt a little CAKE for themselves. It reminds me that our choices matter—not just for us, but for the communities we touch.

A Life That Feeds the Soul

At the end of the day, living the CAKE mantra is about feeding the soul. It's about creating a life that is rich, satisfying, and uniquely mine. It's about savoring the sweetness, even amidst the mess. It's about trusting that connection, authenticity, kindness, and evolution will carry me through whatever comes next.

I am still learning. Still stumbling. Still baking new cakes and trying new ingredients. But I am doing it with a full heart, a curious mind, and the deep conviction that this—this imperfect, evolving, CAKE-filled life—is more than enough.

Chapter 15: Looking Forward: Sustaining Change and Welcoming the Future

The end of a journey, I now realize, is never really an ending. It's a pause—a breath—a chance to look back with gratitude and forward with hope. As I sit down to write this final chapter, Lucy curled at my feet and a fresh mug of coffee warming my hands, I feel the familiar blend of excitement and uncertainty that always comes with the prospect of new beginnings.

When I first set out on this path, all I wanted was relief: from grief, from burnout, from the relentless pressure to be perfect and pleasing. I couldn't have imagined how much more awaited me—not just healing, but transformation. Not just survival, but a kind of thriving I'd never known before. The rituals, the boundaries, the compassion, the community, the CAKE—they've become the scaffolding of a new life, sturdy and flexible, ready to hold whatever I choose to build next.

The Work of Sustaining Change

Sustaining change is its own act of courage. In the past, I treated transformation as a one-time event—a dramatic leap into the unknown, followed by a swift return to "normal." But true change, I've learned, is quieter and more persistent. It's a daily practice, a series of choices, a willingness to keep showing up for myself and my values, even when the old patterns beckon me back.

There are mornings when I still want to hit snooze on my rituals, evenings when I'm tempted to numb out with snacks or screens, days when Evelyn, my inner critic, is louder than Evie, my inner bestie. But now I know how to be a safe space. I know how to forgive myself and begin again. I know that progress is rarely linear, and that each small, imperfect step is a victory.

What sustains me most is the clarity of my "why." I want a life filled with connection, authenticity, kindness, and evolution—not just for myself, but for my clients, my neighbors, my friends, and anyone else who crosses my path. The CAKE mantra is no longer just a tool for healing; it's a compass for living.

Welcoming the Future with Openness

If Italy taught me to savor the present, and Lucy taught me to embrace connection, then this chapter is about trusting the future—a future I can't predict or control, but can greet with openness and curiosity.

I don't know exactly what lies ahead. There may be new adventures, new heartbreaks, new opportunities to grow. There will certainly be more mornings to nourish, more evenings to reflect, more boundaries to draw and redraw as I continue to evolve. There will be days when I stumble and days when I soar. Through it all, I plan to keep asking: What is the kindest, most authentic, most connected, most growth-minded choice I can make today?

I hope to deepen my coaching practice, expanding my ability to hold space for others as they navigate their own transformations. I want to keep building community—both locally and globally—by sharing my story, my struggles, and my small daily joys. I want to keep learning, keep softening, keep stretching into new possibilities.

And I want to keep living with Lucy as my guide—her tail wagging, her heart open, her invitation to play and connect always at the ready.

Creating a Legacy of CAKE

One of the most beautiful surprises of this journey has been witnessing the ripple effect of small, intentional change. The neighbor who now greets me with a smile and an update about her own dog. The client who embraces self-compassion for the first time. The friend who starts a new morning ritual because she saw how it grounded me. These are tiny legacies, seeds planted in ordinary moments, growing into something larger than any one of us.

I want my legacy to be one of CAKE—a life that feeds others as much as it feeds me. A life that models the messy, imperfect courage of showing up. A life that invites others to put down their burdens, even for a moment, and savor the sweetness that's available right now.

A Note to My Future Self

If I could send a message into the future, it would be this:

Keep noticing the wonder. Keep playing. Keep risking vulnerability, even when it feels scary. Remember that it's always okay to begin again. Trust that you are enough—not because of what you do, but because of who you are.

Let connection guide you. Let authenticity ground you. Let kindness soften you. Let evolution inspire you. And when in doubt, eat the cake, walk the dog, and welcome whatever comes next with an open heart.

The Journey Continues

As I close this chapter, I am filled not with certainty, but with hope. The journey is ongoing, the learning never ends. But I have everything I need to meet whatever comes—the rituals, the community, the compassion, the courage, and, above all, the sweet, sustaining mantra of CAKE.

So here's to the next adventure, to the next morning, to the next small, brave step. Here's to you, dear reader, and whatever your next chapter may hold. May you find your own CAKE—connection, authenticity, kindness, and evolution—and may it nourish you, now and always.

With gratitude and love,

Elaina

Acknowledgments

No journey of healing and growth happens in isolation, and this book is the culmination of love, encouragement, and wisdom generously shared by so many. I am deeply grateful for every person, experience, and quiet moment that helped bring these pages to life.

To my husband Jay, whose steadfast love and understanding has been my roots and my shelter. Thank you for believing in me, even when I doubted myself, and for giving me space to become who I am.

To my friends, near and far, who listened without judgment, cheered me on in moments of doubt, and brought laughter into even the hardest days. Your presence—whether in person, in texts, or across continents—reminded me of the healing power of true connection.

To my clients and the entire coaching community: You entrusted me with your stories and your vulnerability, and in doing so, you inspired my own courage. Thank you for allowing me to witness your journeys and for teaching me that growth is always possible, no matter where we begin.

To my neighbors, who became companions in both the ordinary and the extraordinary. Your kindness turned a street into a community and helped me rediscover the joy of belonging.

To all who have walked alongside me on the path of recovery, self-discovery, and evolution—whether through shared conversations, book recommendations, workshops, or simple acts of kindness—your influence is woven throughout these chapters.

To my fellow coaches, teachers, mentors, and guides, both formal and informal, who helped me see the world (and myself) with new eyes. Your wisdom is the invisible thread holding these lessons together.

A special thank you to Lucy, my King Charles Cavalier, whose joy and beauty are a daily reminder to play, to love, and to greet the world with an open heart. You have introduced me to neighbors, to laughter, and to more moments of delight than I can count. You are, quite simply, the best four-legged coauthor a person could wish for.

And finally, to the places that changed me—Italy, with your slow magic and ancient beauty, and my own neighborhood, with your quiet promise of community and new beginnings. Thank you for teaching me that healing is everywhere, if we are willing to look for it.

To everyone who picks up this book: thank you for letting my story become a part of yours. May you find your own CAKE—connection, authenticity, kindness, and evolution—wherever your journey takes you.

With deepest gratitude,

Elaina

Stay Tuned

This story is just the beginning. Florida has a way of sticking to you—its heat, its wildness, the way the past hides under the surface like cypress roots in dark water. What you've read here only scratches at the memories, the mischief, and the lessons that shaped growing up under that big southern sky.

The next chapter of this journey is on its way. Expect more sun-drenched afternoons, more tangled friendships, and stories that don't always stay pretty once the lights go out. If you've ever wondered what it really means to come of age in a place where hurricanes and summer crushes roll in just as fast—you'll want to keep turning the pages when the next book arrives.

Let's Keep in Touch

I'd love to hear from you—your own memories, your stories, the way a certain song or a summer storm might take you back, too. You can find updates about upcoming releases, bonus stories, and behind-the-scenes notes by connecting with me here:

Website: MentalFitnessToday.com

Etsy Shop: Bourne Creatives

Pinterest: pinterest.com/mentalfitnesstoday

Substack: mentalfitness247.substack.com/

Every story gets bigger when it's shared, and I can't wait to share what's next with you.